When in Doubt, Lead!
Part 3

The Leader's Guide to a Focused and Empowered Workforce

By
Dennis Compton

Published by
Fire Protection Publications
Oklahoma State University
2002

ISBN #0-87939-205-3
Library of Congress Control Number 2001012345

First Edition   2 3 4 5 6 7 8 9 10
Printed in the United States of America

Design and Layout by Desa Porter

Contact us for more information about Fire Protection Publications at Oklahoma State University, headquarters of International Fire Service Training Association:
          Send email to editors@osufpp.org
          Phone (405) 744-5723
          Write to 930 North Willis, OSU, Stillwater, OK 74078
          Or see our web page at www.ifsta.org.

.... Table of Contents ....

.... Dedication ....

To the members of the Mesa and Phoenix Fire Departments in Arizona...you are great people and a pleasure to know, learn from, and work with. Thanks for everything you've done for me over the years.

In memory of my friends and the many other firefighters who lost their lives at the World Trade Center in New York City on September 11, 2001. God bless all the members of the fire service. God bless America.

.... Preface ....

Organizations continually work to create an atmosphere that results in the successful delivery of the mission. This involves much more than simply assigning work to people and waiting for them to perform. Exceptional organizations did not reach that status by chance: they were able to capture some critical concepts that tend to consistently move people's performance toward excellence. Understanding the system within which we lead and manage is basic to our individual and collective success. Those who occupy formal positions of leadership-the supervisors at various levels-represent one of the key elements. They act as living examples of what the organization claims as its values; they motivate, coach, and supervise those within their span of control; and they continually act as a conduit between those who direct the organization overall and the individual workers. In the eyes of the individual workers, the supervisors, especially those in decentralized organizations like fire departments, can actually "become the organization." The workers assume that the behavior and performance of the supervisor reflect the expectations of senior management. They are affected behaviorally and psychologically by the example set by the supervisor...good or bad. The organizational investment made in the supervisors will have as much or more impact on the quality of workforce performance as any other issue.

Another key is understanding and institutionalizing the concept of self-discipline. The anchor point of any successful disciplinary philosophy is self-discipline...this has been a component of every class or book covering employee discipline that we have ever been exposed to. However, the term "self-discipline" is not universally defined. In fact, the definition is so vague that individual employees can basically interpret it to mean whatever they wish. Defining, teaching, and following-up on the expectation of self-discipline is another key to organizational focus, empowerment, and excellence.

The formal structure of any organization is important to document, publish, and communicate. It serves many purposes including identifying work responsibilities, financial accounting processes, reporting relationships, and other important organizational needs. However, a rigid organizational structure can work against the mission and the participation of the workforce when it dictates the way the organization actually operates on a day-to-day basis. Communicating a desired operational structure is of equal importance to the organizational structure. This operational structure serves to define the expectations and focus of the day-to-day operation of the organization...more dynamic, less rigid, more participative, with significantly enhanced communications. Both structures (organizational and operational) serve important purposes.

Empowering work groups and individuals throughout the organization is a philosophy that has grown more common over time. An important issue, however, relates to how one accomplishes empowerment while still providing adequate focus and direction for the organization as a whole. Sometimes people describe direction and empowerment as being in conflict with each other, but that is not the case. Management can (by defining organizational anchors and exercising leadership) provide adequate focus and direction to keep the organization moving forward as a whole while encouraging empowered behavior on the part of individuals and work groups. This requires the cultivation of an energized work environment with excellent leadership and management direction designed to tie the efforts of all component parts into one "system."

This book captures these key concepts and describes each as an individual piece of the whole. An organization cannot excel without achieving excellence in the areas of:

- Cultivating supervisory leadership
- Understanding the system
- Defining and instilling self-discipline
- Defining organizational and operational structures
- Balancing management direction and organizational focus with empowerment

I hope these concepts are communicated in a simple format that, when combined with the other books in the When in Doubt, Lead! series, provides managers and supervisors (our formal leadership) with a unique methodology designed to make their organization more effective. Enjoy this book...its goal is to make people more effective... individually and collectively.

.... Chapter One ....
A Systems Approach to Managing Fire and Life Safety Services

Introduction

Many separate (yet interrelated) component parts comprise a systems approach to providing effective fire and life safety services. Managers today must pay attention to all components of the fire and life safety equation, avoiding the temptation to focus only on areas within which they have expertise or interest, or that are politically popular. When the focus is narrow, the overall system weakens, resulting in a negative impact on the mission.

One of the arts of managing a fire department, or for that matter any organization, is coming to the realization that everything in the system is connected to everything else. It is impossible to address (or ignore) any one aspect of the system without impacting one or more other component parts. This applies whether the work group is career, volunteer, or a combination of both. Exceptional fire service leaders and managers know that they are guiding a system...with the whole of the process being only as strong as the weakest part. As this concept is embraced by fire service managers, it can be effectively communicated to influential people outside the fire service. The members of fire departments, and those in all other fire service organizations, provide a variety of line services and support functions within the overall mission. Each element is important and requires attention when building an exceptional fire and life safety system and guiding that system toward the future.

The Mission

Everything we read or hear today about managing organizations tells us that to be effective we must know what business we're in and become the best we can be at that business. Interviews with customers who have received emergency services from their fire departments reveal a perspective on our business that we must come to understand, and throughout our careers, never forget.

When asked to think back, many customers say that the day they had to call the fire department for an emergency response was either one of the worst days of their life or the worst day of their life. That is a unique relationship to have with one's customers. According to them, we (the entire fire service) are in the "worst-day-of-their-life" business. Fire service managers who accept this fact realize that they must manage each element of the fire and life safety system as if it were in place to address the worst day of someone's life...because our customers believe that it is. Any weak element of the system can produce a negative outcome for customers on their "worst day."

The System

In this day and age, emphasis is placed on building sound infrastructures within our communities. It is understood that infrastructures addressing transportation, water, sewers, other utilities, communications, parks, and so forth are critical to a community's quality of life and viability. This same concept applies directly to the fire and life safety infrastructure of a community. Fire service managers are responsible for building a community infrastructure that is directed toward preventing the worst day of someone's life from occurring in the first place; teaching people how to prevent it or how to survive that worst day, should it occur; building an emergency response element designed to provide fast, skillful, and caring service; designing support systems (internal and external) to maintain quality service delivery programs; developing positive relationships, and providing the human and physical resources required to do so. Unless each of these system components receives adequate, ongoing attention from fire service managers and community leaders, the fire and life safety infrastructure of the community is compromised and may not be effective in addressing the "worst day" of a particular customer's life. This fire and life safety infrastructure is critical to protecting life, property, history, memorabilia, and the economic stability of the community and our nation.

An Illustration: The Stool

Someone once said that a picture is worth a thousand words. Assuming that's true, an illustration might effectively demonstrate the various component parts of the fire and life safety infrastructure...the "system." An effective illustration is a three-legged stool. To be useful at all, the stool must be made of a substantial material. Each part of the stool (the seat, legs, and braces) is totally dependent on the other parts for strength, or the stool is unstable and cannot be used. It will not support the weight being applied to it and will fail at some point.

As a symbol of a systems approach to managing fire and life safety services, the stool is an excellent illustration. This stool is made from the most important resource in the organization...the people. This includes the members of the fire department, related organizations, board members, community managers, and public officials. The quality of the material from which the stool is made is reflected in these people's levels of commitment, competence, ethics, diversity, and compassion for the external customers and each other. Their individual and collective capabilities determine the basic strength of the stool.

The weight of the fire and life safety mission rests on the seat of the stool. The stool must be strong enough to support the entire weight of the mission. If not, the stool (system) will eventually fail. For most of the fire service, this mission includes protecting the community from fire and a full range of other hazards that can harm people and damage property.

The three legs of the stool represent the line (external) service delivery programs of a fire department: fire prevention, public education, and emergency response. The stool illustrates the equal importance of each of these three primary line services to the effectiveness of the system: strong prevention through consensus-based fire and building codes, including requirements for built-in protection and effective fire investigation; an all-risk approach to public education; and an emergency response component designed to deliver a full range of emergency services. Each of the three legs of the stool is equally important and represents a critical component of the fire and life safety infrastructure of a community.

The braces represent the staff (internal) elements of the system. They are in place to support the effectiveness of the line services and the members who provide those services. The braces are critical to the strength, stability, and effectiveness of the stool (the system). Without the braces, the legs alone will not provide enough stability to support the full weight of the fire and life safety mission.

Fire Prevention

Fire prevention services are line services provided to customers in our communities. A full set of consensus-based fire and building codes, as well as, standards that incorporate current performance requirements and practices form the foundation for a built environment that minimizes the negative effect of fires, explosions, terrorism, and other events that occur.

Fire and Life Safety Mission

Fire Prevention (Codes)

Emergency Response

Public Education (Risk Watch®)

Training and Preparation

Members and System Support

Partnerships, Relationships, and Politics

Infrastructure and Equipment

Fire service leaders must advocate and protect the true consensus process for developing and approving codes and standards. The National Fire Protection Association (NFPA) offers the most comprehensive set of codes available. The process for developing these codes is certified by the American National Standards Institute (ANSI).

Codes cannot be effective unless compliance inspections are conducted during construction, and periodic follow-up inspections are performed throughout the life of the structure or facility. Fire departments utilize a variety of approaches to ensure compliance with codes, including conducting fire investigations to determine the causes of actual fires.

Built-in protection, such as automatic fire sprinklers, is key to protecting life and property, as well as maintaining the economic stability of our communities. The future must include a greater emphasis on the installation of fire sprinklers in homes. A home fire sprinkler system is an effective tool for protecting life and property from the devastation of fire. Over 80 percent of the people who die in fires each year die in their homes. Much of the property lost in residential fires has immeasurable sentimental value and simply cannot be replaced. The frequency and severity of residential fires could be dramatically reduced in the future if new home construction included automatic fire sprinklers and incentives were offered to encourage retro-fitting existing homes with fire sprinklers. We must make this a priority in the future...and set the example by installing fire sprinklers in our own homes.

The stool cannot support the weight of the overall fire and life safety mission without a strong fire prevention leg designed to maintain the safety of existing structures and facilities, as well as to build safer communities in the future. People sometimes survive a tragedy because of fire, structural, and other safety considerations required in buildings. Whether addressing safety in structures, facilities, or regulating hazardous contents or cargoes, these codes are an investment in the long-term fire and life safety infrastructure of our communities and represent an equally important line service delivery program within the system.

Public Education

All-risk public education programs represent another critical line service provided to customers by fire departments. These include school-based programs, programs targeted at high-risk groups within the population, and general education programs provided for the community at

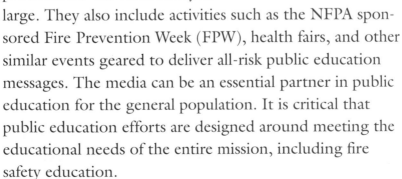

large. They also include activities such as the NFPA sponsored Fire Prevention Week (FPW), health fairs, and other similar events geared to deliver all-risk public education messages. The media can be an essential partner in public education for the general population. It is critical that public education efforts are designed around meeting the educational needs of the entire mission, including fire safety education.

When implementing a school-based all-risk public education program, the most comprehensive delivery tool is NFPA's Risk Watch® Program. Risk Watch® is easily incorporated into the school curriculum with minimal additional impact on time commitments by the teachers, the fire department, or other partners. Approximately 80 percent of the Risk Watch® learning objectives correlate directly to existing school and educational requirements for health, language arts, and physical education in each state in the country.

Risk Watch® is designed for preschool through eighth grade and addresses unintentional-injury prevention by incorporating the following eight lessons within a series of five modules:

1. Motor vehicle safety

2. Fire and burn prevention

3. Choking, suffocation, and strangulation prevention

4. Poisoning prevention

5. Falls prevention

6. Firearms injury prevention

7. Bike and pedestrian safety

8. Water safety

Intentional injury prevention and disaster preparedness education may also be integrated into Risk Watch® in the future.

The Risk Watch® model is based on building community coalitions and does not rely solely on the fire department for its success. The fire department is a key partner, and in some cases the catalyst behind the program, but other agencies with related missions can also be involved. One advantage of Risk Watch® is that it is fully developed and readily transferable to any system for implementation. Therefore, the local organizations do not incur the overhead costs associated with curriculum development, validation, revision, or the production of materials necessary to teach the core program. They are all available from NFPA, as are a variety of other aids on the NFPA website.

Public education programs designed for the general population and high-risk groups are also critical program components. All-risk public education targeted to the very young, the elderly, and the disabled are examples of such efforts. The NFPA Center for High-Risk Outreach is a leader and a resource for guidance in these efforts. NFPA's "Remembering When" program, designed specifically around burn and fall prevention for the elderly, is but one example.

All-risk public education is a line service delivery component of the fire and life safety infrastructure of a community and represents an equally important leg of the stool. Without a strong public education leg, the stool cannot support the full weight of the mission. Education adds knowledge, changes behavior, and helps individuals act out their roles as members of society in preventing harm to themselves and others. People sometimes prevent or survive a tragedy because of information or behaviors they learned through fire and life safety educational sessions. As any firefighter would say, "The greatest rescue was the one we didn't have to make...the customers either prevented the event or got themselves out of the situation safely before our arrival because of something they had learned prior to the incident."

Emergency Response

Emergency response is the next critical service delivery component of the system. This leg of the stool is just as important as the other two. When customers dial 9-1-1, they expect service that is fast, performed skillfully, and provided by firefighters who care about them, their loved ones, and their property. This emergency response leg of the stool includes fires, medical emergencies, hazardous materials incidents, technical rescue situations, terrorist acts, and a variety of service calls addressing many issues and needs in our communities.

Deploying and dispatching resources for emergency response is a critical fire department responsibility. An emergency response system that is not properly located, staffed, trained, and equipped will fail to provide adequate service on the "worst day" that an individual (or the community, or nation as a whole) experiences. Whether the emergency response workforce of the system is career, volunteer, combination, industrial, public, or private, accessing the resources must be quick and easy for the customer. The emergency response component of the system must be focused on delivering service...period.

That is the only reason this leg of the stool exists. Some-times people survive a tragedy only because of the capability of the firefighters who respond to rescue and protect them. It has to be performed right every time. After all, the system is responding to the worst day in people's lives...many times...each day.

The emergency response menu of services has expanded significantly and will continue to shift in the future. Without a strong emergency response component the stool is not strong enough to support the full weight of the mission.

Support Components

The support components of the system brace the legs of the stool and are critical to its overall stability. These typically make-up the staff responsibilities of a fire department including:

- Training and preparation

- Member and system support

- Partnerships, relationships, and politics

- Infrastructure and equipment

Training and Preparation

The level of training (the organization's ability to prepare members to perform their roles) is critical to meeting the daily requirements of the external and internal customers and, to a large extent, drives the organization's ability to change and develop. Key to all persons' effectiveness is to know what is expected of them and to be trained to perform to those expectations. Training and preparation must not only be directed at those who deliver emergency services. It must include all members of the department: those in prevention, public education and emergency response, as well as, those who work in support of the line service providers. The International Fire Service Training Association (IFSTA), based at Oklahoma State University, offers the most comprehensive set of validated training materials designed to meet the needs of the fire service.

People play like they practice. If addressing a particular issue of performance, a change to the process, an added service, a shift in culture, or any other issue dealing with human behavior, training and preparation are key to a successful system and represent an important brace of the stool.

Member and System Support

Adequate support from the standpoint of basic human resource management is critical to the stool's stability and the system's effectiveness. Fair compensation, an emphasis on safety, medical and chemical exposure management, an Incident Management System (IMS), standard operating procedures (SOPs), and incorporating humane supervisory, management, and leadership practices are some of the more common elements of this important brace...and there are many more.

System support includes ensuring that members have a clear understanding of the organization's vision, mission, and values. It also includes short- and long-range planning, as well as the ability to bring those plans to life within the organization. This is critical if we expect our people to stay committed to the mission and function in a positive, productive, and healthy manner. This single component of the stool impacts the strength and stability (the effectiveness) of the other legs and braces more than any other.

Partnerships, Relationships, and Politics

It is difficult for organizations to achieve anything that is community based without forming partnerships with others who share their vision or have similar missions. Community coalitions and partnerships formed for advocating or implementing specific programs (like Risk Watch®) can be used for many other purposes as well.

A department's internal and external relationships have a tremendous impact on its overall performance. Simply stated, negative personal or organizational relationships can (and do) interfere with the mission. This impact must be minimized.

Also, if a fire department lacks the ability to be politically effective it will struggle to get or keep required resources. Leaders who struggle with politics usually struggle with other basic areas of management and leadership as well. Community involvement is critical to a fire department's community image and standing. On a national level, the Congressional Fire Services Institute (CFSI) has developed into a very influential leadership group. It is important that the fire service supports them in their efforts to work with others at the federal level to better meet the needs of our service. Exploring mission-related ways of positively and actively participating with others has a significant impact on our effectiveness.

This critical brace (partnerships, relationships, and politics) will strengthen the service delivery and support components of the system and, therefore, enable the stool to better support the weight of the fire and life safety mission.

Infrastructure and Equipment

This final brace of the stool addresses the infrastructure and equipment necessary to successfully deliver the mission. This is the "hardware" side of the system rather than the "human" side. It includes acquiring and maintaining a myriad of resources such as facilities, real estate, apparatus, equipment, tools, communications and dispatch systems, public education props, safe houses, fire-sprinkler demonstration units, commodities, supplies, technology, E-business, and so forth. This brace of the stool includes the "things" the organization needs to effectively accomplish the mission. It is just as important to the system as any other part of the stool.

Summary

The stool illustrates the overall investment a community should make in the fire and life safety mission of their fire department. Everything a fire department does fits nicely into the systems model that the stool illustrates. Everything is connected to everything else; no element of the system functions totally independent of the other parts. Although

it isn't possible to give each leg and brace 100 percent of the attention that each needs at all times, it is important that each receives sufficient attention (in the form of resources, management, and leadership) so that the stability of the stool is not compromised to the point of system failure. After all, in a given situation, who can predict which leg will save a life? Will lives be saved due to a specific code feature that provided people with the time necessary to evacuate in an emergency or that was incorporated into a structure that prevented a fire from extending to an area of the building where lives would certainly have been lost? Will a life be saved because a 10-year-old child was taught a Risk Watch® class that resulted in her administering the Heimlich maneuver to her 7-year-old brother when he was choking? Will lives be saved due to physical rescues from burning buildings or skillful and timely extrications of people from car crashes that enable them to quickly receive emergency treatment? The fact is each of these line service delivery components (legs) saves lives, and the staff support areas (braces) ensure that members of organizations are properly trained, supported, positioned, connected, and equipped to do so.

A strong system will support the full weight of the fire and life safety mission within the community. A weak or neglected part of the system negatively impacts overall effectiveness.

As fire departments continue to expand prevention, public education, and emergency response services, our support programs must be developed as well. The fire and life safety mission of fire departments will continue to change as we move to the future. We need only look at the events since September 11, 2001 to see one clear example of this reality...but it was also true beforehand. We shouldn't reduce our emphasis on fire safety. We should instead increase the emphasis on the other life safety pieces of the all-risk equation. We shouldn't de-emphasize or reduce our fire fighting and rescue capabilities. We should instead increase our effectiveness in the full range of emergency response services. It's not an either-or choice-it's a system of component parts that we, as fire service managers and leaders, have been entrusted with building and supporting...now and into the future.

This stool illustrates a system designed around the entire mission: prevention, all-risk public education, and emergency response, as well as the support programs necessary to make those services effective at every point of contact with a customer. Fire departments and other fire service organizations are in place to prevent, educate, or respond to the worst day of our customers' lives and must do so effectively every time. If the customers were our own loved ones, that is the least we would expect or accept. The fire service has a proud legacy of commitment and bravery in carrying this out.

Working in the fire service (career or volunteer) is a special calling. We have a unique relationship with our customers and the community as a whole. The stool represents a system designed to build and maintain the fire and life safety infrastructure of a community. Remember that everything in the process is in some way connected to everything else. The stool is always under construction...as it should be.

.... Chapter Two ....
The Fire Officer Is a Leader

A Positive and Productive Fire Officer

We begin our fire service careers with a fire burning in our bellies and with the intent of being around for a long time. The challenges of life at home and at work confront all of us and sometimes make it difficult to keep that fire from dimming over the years.

We've all known fire officers with a lot of seniority who are as positive and fulfilled as they were in the very beginning of their careers...and we've seen situations in which officers (new and old) were not. They may be unhappy with the work they're doing, the changes in the fire service since they started, or with their departments, their bosses, and sometimes even their friends and family.

The demeanor of company officers and their outlook on things in general have a tremendous impact on other members and on service delivery. Working for a specific officer can be the best or worst thing that can happen in a member's career...and the impact can be long lasting.

Teamwork

Many fire officers have provided me with suggestions for helping other officers remain positive, productive examples for members to model. The following represents some thoughts on this issue:

- Fire officers should strive to approach their duties with the same teamwork-based attitude that they naturally utilized in the beginning of their careers. Maintaining a sense of self-motivation that is directed toward competence, safety, learning, teaching, and overall wellness is an important part of that process.

- As long as we're involved in the fire service, we should remain students of the fire service. This could include attending a seminar periodically, taking classes, reading, sharing information with other members, or transferring our experiences through storytelling to provide opportunities for others to learn and grow professionally.

- Officers who are consistent and predictable make it easier for others to interact with them, and they also are better able to maintain their sense of direction as supervisors. Being as fair as possible, avoiding the appearance of favoritism, displaying trust in other members, being honest in our interactions with others, and simply being nice to the people we encounter can be daily "booster shots" to a fire officer's sense of self-worth and value, thus affecting their overall demeanor in a positive way.

- Being good coaches and working on our communications skills can help avoid personnel issues that can get us down. Confronting issues in a productive way is preferred to letting them fester until emotions get the best of us...sometimes resulting in negative, long-lasting reactions among those who were involved.

- As much as possible, fire officers should stay focused on the mission, committed to service delivery, and concerned about the welfare of their crew members. Supporting the organization, buying into the future, and setting a positive example can be contagious when modeled by the leader.

- Approaching each emergency call or work assignment with the eagerness and empathy that we displayed early in our careers can help keep spirits high. Encouraging participation and input from crew members in prevention, public education, and support programs helps the fire officer create an environment in which the work is taken seriously and the workers have fun doing it. A positive work environment creates positive, productive people-including the supervisor.

- Although this is difficult, officers should not allow bad things that happen at home to dominate the work environment, nor should they let difficult times at work create barriers to family relationships at home. That concept is a lot easier to write than it is to do, but officers who give it periodic thought will manage this balance better than those who pay no attention to it at all.

Staying The Course

We are all subject to up- and down-cycles at work and at home. An important question to consider is, "Are there specific, realistic behaviors and concepts that we can practice to help us stay positive, productive, and healthy contributors for the entire duration of our career?" The answer is "yes." I know many fire officers who do this very well and have been a great influence on the careers of others. They have found a way to keep the fire in their belly lit, which can sustain or reignite the fire in others. We all know that this can have a positive effect on service delivery in the streets, businesses, and school classrooms, as well as on internal relations.

Most of us plan to be around for a long time, so we may as well be effective, enjoy ourselves, and help those around us do the same. This is important at all levels of the organization.

Safety Leadership by Fire Officers

I often ask fire officers (past ones, current ones, new ones, and wannabees) to contemplate their role in maintaining a safety-conscious attitude and safe practices among their crew at the fire station, during training, and at emergency scenes.

They sometimes articulate some specific (realistic) behaviors or approaches that a fire officer could use that would assist them in accomplishing this goal. Following is some of the feedback I've received:

- All members should be encouraged to be team players and held accountable for their actions.

- An overall positive work environment can help create a safe work environment.

- Fire officers must do their part to create trust within the work group.

- Fire officers should be attentive at all times. They must stay alert and try to see the big picture to enhance overall workplace and emergency scene safety.

- Be calm and consistent with safety matters and be willing to correct behavior or performance when necessary.

- Be flexible and adaptable. This helps officers to stay open-minded and to accept changes in safety procedures and other regulations. They must be able to be coaches and safety salespersons.

- Training exercises and emergency incidents should be critiqued. Part of the critique should include a review of safety issues, good performance, problems and solutions, as well as other pertinent information.

- Fire officers should be careful not to overwork crews. Rehab should be an important part of the overall work plan.

- Fire officers should ensure that members are aware of safety policies and procedures and that the officers' expectations are in concert with the fire department's. This should be communicated clearly to minimize confusion and improve performance. This includes issues such as driving, the use of equipment, and all other aspects of safety.

- Remember that fire officers lead primarily by example. Safety behaviors are just one of the many areas where this applies.

- Fire officers should not compromise safety. There should be a line drawn somewhere when it comes to safety practices, and crossing that line should not be acceptable to the officer.

- Fire officers should be advocates of overall wellness initiatives. This includes medical, physical, emotional, and psychological aspects of the total wellness package.

- Training creates habits (good or bad). People should train in a way that is consistent with how they want to perform in real situations.

- Case studies of actual incidents can be excellent tools for safety training.

- Positive reinforcement and recognition are powerful motivators and can be effective in improving safety practices.

Rather than focusing on what to do with people who don't follow safety procedures, it would probably be more beneficial and productive to reinforce the importance of preventing people from operating outside of our expectations in the first place. We don't do enough officer training on those techniques. Fire officers must do a thorough job of covering the topic of safety. Safety was (and always is) a good place for performance discussions to start.

Fire Officer Leadership: Additional Thoughts

This section focuses on a few of the behaviors that are consistently mentioned when we discuss the subject of fire officer leadership in the fire service. This list is not intended to be all-inclusive, but these behaviors are frequently mentioned by people when they are discussing leadership in the areas of safety, self-discipline, empowerment, and staying a positive, productive and healthy leader throughout a career. They are as follows:

- Always set a positive example and practice sound personal and professional values.

- Share our expectations of others "up front" and encourage people to get involved in their department's issues and processes.

- Good behavior and performance should be rewarded in some way at every opportunity; it should not be taken for granted. Unsatisfactory performance or behavior should never be rewarded; and if it is, expect to see it repeated.

- Consistent with our long-standing fire service tradition, fire officers should be customer focused (externally and internally) and community/neighborhood centered.

- Stay an advocate of the fire department and help other members be successful-including your boss.

- Remain competent in our jobs and value composure as a critical trait of an officer. Help people stay trained and help each member grow professionally.

- Display a high regard for safety, including physical, psychological and emotional wellness.

- Practice self-discipline and expect the same from others. Be willing and able to impose corrective discipline when necessary.

- Remember the five L's. A friend shared them with me years ago. They are good for the soul and can help focus and balance leaders:

Never stop Learning.

Love our friends and family.

Believe in the value of Labor as a motivator.

Laugh often.

Know when it's time to Leave...but leave something behind for others.

- As a fire officer, decide what you would like others to say about working for you, then pursue a course to make that vision become a reality. It helps for us to know what we (as individuals) really stand for as leaders...but we should probably keep that list short.

As leaders there is nothing more important than providing support to the members who perform the mission every day. Remember that our mission has three critical service delivery responsibilities; prevention, all-risk public education, and emergency response. Fire officers play a key leadership role and act as conduits that connect the organizational support to the services...and thus service to the customers.

I don't know anyone capable of meeting everyone's leadership expectations and needs everyday, but the more thought we give to basic leadership concepts, the closer we will come to that goal. We must willingly review the issue of leadership and its relationship to safety, as well as external and internal service delivery. We are very fortunate to have so many capable fire officers in our systems who do this so well.

Chapter Three

Keys to Self-Discipline at the Company Level

Self-Discipline in a Fire Company

People who evaluate organizational behavior and health say that the anchor point for discipline in a work group is self-discipline. Yet for some reason, from an organizational perspective, we are reluctant to define what self-discipline really means. At the core of self-discipline is the belief that most people are basically driven to behave and perform in a way that is consistent with the organization's expectations. Most would agree that this assumption not only has merit but is a key to effectively managing and leading any group.

Maintaining a self-disciplined atmosphere should be a priority for any supervisor. It is also critical that supervisors be willing and able to impose corrective, progressive, and lawful disciplinary actions when it becomes necessary to do so. We have all witnessed work settings where both elements were present (self-discipline and imposed discipline) and we have seen work settings where one or both were absent. There are definitive results present in both of these atmospheres.

A large number of current and future company officers were asked to identify specific (realistic) behaviors or approaches they could use to create an atmosphere in which self-discipline could flourish and imposed discipline could be used as a positive, productive tool when necessary. Following are the thoughts and suggestions of those who responded to this issue:

- Crew members and the company officer must accept and share responsibility for creating a positive, productive atmosphere based on the concept of self-discipline. To do so, the crew members must have a clear understanding of the officer's expectations...up front.

- The company officer should empower crew members to participate in decision-making when planning the daily routine and workload. The company officer should assign projects based on each person's capabilities and talents whenever possible. This will help maintain the interest of crew members. Know the strengths of the group and utilize them, but also know each member's individual limitations. One of the keys to effective delegation is timely follow-up.

- Setting a positive example and displaying a sincere willingness to listen and learn are important to the company officer. Empathetic listening, flexibility, and encouraging members to provide input into issues within the company help establish an environment rich with self-motivation and self-discipline.

- Building a sense of trust and mutual respect within the crew supports the concept of self-discipline on the part of crew members.

- Crew members feel that a company officer who is organized, consistent, and somewhat predictable promotes self-discipline. When leadership is present, expectations are clear, and standard operating procedures are followed, the need for imposed discipline is minimized.

- When it is necessary to impose discipline, the focus should be to correct behavior and improve performance. When it is simply intended as a punitive measure, imposed discipline is not usually effective and many times has a negative overall effect on the individual and the work group as a whole.

- A company officer must identify whether a particular problem with behavior or performance of a crew member is related to training that should be provided or to a disregard for known rules or standards. Making this distinction will provide considerable guidance to the company officer in handling the situation and achieving a positive outcome.

- The fact that there will be consequences for unsatisfactory behavior or performance should be clear within the fire company. When appropriate to do so, incidents should be properly documented in a way that is consistent with the department's disciplinary procedures.

- An important component of developing our members is career counseling. Maintaining continuing education programs and monitoring people's progress can contribute significantly to an atmosphere of self-discipline.

- Other helpful practices include using public praise that reinforces positive behavior, providing timely feedback on overall performance, and avoiding the appearance of favoritism. When there is a need to counsel or constructively criticize, do so privately.

I'm sure you can think of other practices that have been successful in helping to maintain a self-disciplined fire company and successfully imposing discipline when there is the need to do so. If so, perhaps you should write them down and share them with others. I'm always impressed with how much fire officers really know about motivation, self-discipline, and addressing corrective action in the fire company.

The ability to balance these issues of discipline on an individual basis impacts the performance of the group and the quality of service. That alone provides sufficient reason to make it a priority. This section was not intended to cover all of the elements that come to mind, but these serve as excellent reminders and could be useful.

"Running Your Own" Fire Station

No matter where we go in the fire service, a message that company officers consistently communicate within a fire department is that they want to have the latitude to "run their own" fire stations. I don't blame them, I wanted the same thing when I was a company officer.

It might be interesting to identify some of the key indicators that are present when a fire company is well supervised, has good leadership, and can function with minimal daily outside direction from a chief officer. In other words, to define what it looks like when company officers are "running their own" fire station. The following indicators have been gathered over several years of interaction and discussion with company and chief officers from several fire departments and are intended to form that definition:

- Each crew member understands that the purpose of the fire department is to serve the customers; through fire prevention, public education, emergency response, and a full range of internal and external support services.

- The crew looks good and is appropriately dressed. Uniforms are in good condition and the members wear the appropriate uniform for the work being performed at a given time.

- The station, apparatus, and equipment are kept clean and in good working order, not because a chief is coming to inspect, but because that is what is expected of the fire company in that station.

- Losing equipment is a "big deal" within the company, and the regular loss of equipment is not acceptable.

- Reports and other paperwork are completed in an accurate and timely manner. Administrative files (whether computer-based or paper) are maintained properly. This is done with the understanding that the information will be important to others inside or outside the organization at a later date.

- Coordination and communication between the shifts at the station are open, positive, and productive. Necessary relief-oriented duties are conducted at the beginning and end of each shift to avoid confusion within the station among the work shifts.

- The crew members perform their work in a positive, effective manner and do not spend an inordinate amount of time complaining about their jobs, the fire department, or each other. When a question or issue arises that the company officer cannot address, it is pursued appropriately through the system. The crew members display pride in their work, the organization, and each other.

- The company members adhere to the department rules and regulations without the need for substantial supervision from inside or outside the fire company. They have a positive attitude and approach to issues like sick leave use, safety, wellness, utility usage, and the care of fire department property and equipment.

- The crew uses discretion and sound judgment concerning activities in the fire station. Members are conscious of the appearance or potential impact of issues like the use of beds at inappropriate times; the playing of video or computer games; materials, signs, or remarks on walls, lockers, or bulletin boards; television use and general horseplay.

- Time is used in a productive manner. In busy companies, this could include a safety nap so that the crew will be alert for the entire duration of the shift. It also includes pre-fire planning, training, prevention, public education, maintenance programs, and other activities.

- The crew performs competently at emergency incidents and follows the department's standard operating procedures (SOPs).

- Personal visitors to the fire stations are received only at appropriate hours. The crew members consciously recognize all visitors who come to the station and have a positive attitude toward visitors from other fire departments, other agencies, and all visitors in general.

- Company members attempt to understand how people outside the fire department might perceive what they (the crew members) might be doing at a given time. Activities that appear OK to fire department members might not be viewed that way by others. This can damage the image of the fire department. Although this can be difficult to address, it is extremely important that the crew members are sensitive to this issue and that crew members help each other with it. Physical fitness activities and shopping are two excellent examples of activities easily misunderstood by the public.

- When problems occur in the fire company, they are dealt with appropriately by the company officer. Chief officers outside the fire company should not have to cause this to occur or have to handle company level issues on a regular basis.

We regularly use words like ownership, accountability, and empowerment to describe our philosophy toward people in our organizations, but sometimes we struggle to define what those terms really mean. Perhaps these indicators have identified some measurable, realistic steps in that direction. It seems that if company officers are creating an atmosphere where these behaviors are occurring on a regular basis, without requiring daily direction from outside the fire company, then one could say that they are "running their own" fire stations in a way that would make any fire department and community proud of their performance.

We shouldn't cause our boss to have to do our job, nor should our boss interfere with our performance on a day-to-day basis if we are doing what is expected. It becomes easier for company officers and chief officers to operate within this model when fire stations are being "run" in a way that is consistent with the expectations of the department, which are probably somewhat consistent with these indicators. I hope you found these interesting, but more important, I hope you find them useful. I'm glad that people have been willing to share them with each other over time.

.... Chapter Four ....
Organizational and Operational Structures

Introduction

The structure of the organization sets the tone for the way the people inside the system view their roles, the roles of others, the focus of their collective efforts, and how they each (individually) fit into the overall picture. We send a lot of messages through the way we organize our resources, including the way we communicate cultural issues. The way we organize ourselves structurally and the way we want the system to operate structurally might be two different things. In fact, in many progressive organizations, they are. This chapter will discuss organizational and operational structures in a way that clearly defines the two.

Organizational Structure

Basic organizational structures are utilized to organize our resources (see Figure 4-1). They are typically laid out in a hierarchical format that includes:

- The Chief Executive Officer (CEO)
- Functions that report to the CEO
- The major Divisions that report to the CEO
- The Sections that form Divisions and report directly to Division Heads

- Work Units that form Sections and report directly to Section Managers

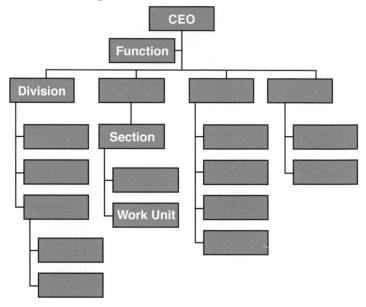

Figure 4-1. Sample organizational structure.

Some claim that the traditional organizational structure is obsolete and serves no useful purpose in the management process. I disagree with that and clearly see the value of the organizational structure to the effectiveness of the people trying to manage, lead, and work inside the system...as well as customers and others trying to access the organization from the outside. There are other benefits as well. The organizational structure also:

- Defines reporting relationships and the chain of command.

- Clarifies the span of control of various managers and supervisors.

- Displays Divisions and Sections that may serve as subunits (or accounts) in the overall budget. In fact, the organizational structure usually accompanies the budget to display these financial and organizational relationships.

- Aligns areas of work and responsibility throughout the organization so that it is clear who is responsible for what work.

There are other benefits of the organizational structure. The problem isn't that we organize ourselves in a standard hierarchical framework...the problems surface when we (day in and day out) operate the organization in that way. Some of the common disadvantages that surface when this happens include:

- Focusing on primarily top-down communications, which creates difficulty getting ideas and issues "up" the organization. It can be very frustrating to function at the "bottom" layers...which in most organizations is where the majority of the workforce exists.

- Creating such rigid organizational lines that territorialism prevails in many decisions.

- Lack of team orientation and a blurred organizational focus. This can result in excessive competition among the Divisions and Sections.

- An unspoken understanding that boxes on the organizational structure translate to status or stature rather than responsibility.

- An organizational climate could be created that leaves the impression that the resources of the organization are in place to service the "top boxes" of the structure rather than to deliver service or products to the internal and external customers.

There are times when a standard, hierarchical structure must be used to direct work, especially in times of crisis. However, these times are the exception. The fact is, most people perform more effectively when the resources are formed into an operational model that is intended to guide the mission and focus resources on the customers.

Operational Structure

The operational structure displays how we should expect the various organizational components to "operate" on a day-to-day basis. The sample operational structure in Figure 4-2 focuses the CEO, Functions, and Divisions on the services provided to customers and the effectiveness of the members who provide those services.

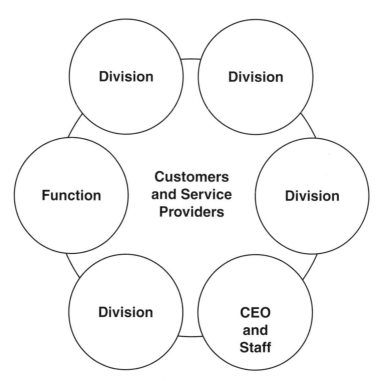

Figure 4-2. Sample operational structure.

The circular structure shows the relationships and interdependence of the organizational elements to one another. It retains areas of responsibility for specific managers and workers; however, it communicates a supportive atmosphere rather than one based upon hierarchy, authority, or control.

It's one thing to draw this operational structure and distribute it to the workforce, but it's another thing to guide the workforce toward making this model come to life. Advantages of the operational structure include:

- Focusing on customer service and making the members as successful as possible in delivering that service.

- Creating more of a partnership among managers and workers throughout the organization.

- Improving organizational communications by causing multidirectional routes of communicating. Workers with customers and among each other; managers with workers; managers among each other...all focusing on improving external and internal customer service.

- Easing the process for members to get ideas and issues into the system for consideration and for the organization to process and implement change.

- Enhancing the concept and the expectation that members of the workforce are empowered to make decisions commensurate to their specific organizational positions and roles.

Instilling such an operational structure can be difficult. Doing so requires people in the organization to accept a different role than what might have been expected in the more traditional hierarchy of a standard organizational structure. Some members of the organization will adapt quickly and easily to these different roles; others will need more time; some may not be able to transition and will require ongoing coaching and direct supervision.

As previously mentioned, the important thing is that the CEO clearly communicates this operational expectation and that leaders reward the workforce at every opportunity for acting within these redefined roles. There will be immediate and short-term benefits, but the long-term improvement in the collective performance of the system as a whole will be nothing short of spectacular. Implementing changes more readily, creating an atmosphere of organizational focus and individual empowerment, and opening lines of communications are critical benefits.

Summary

Organizational and operational structures set the tone for how the people within the organization interact with customers and each other, irrespective of stature or role within the system. Both structures are important to the success of the organization, and when used properly, complement each other very well. It's important that people possess a sense of ownership and responsibility for the area they are specifically assigned to within the organization, but it is just as important that we not let those specific assignments isolate the various organizational areas from each other. The organizational structure is important but the operational structure provides important guidance as well.

The art associated with this concept is to provide organizational focus and direction, which people need, yet to foster an atmosphere of openness and empowerment, which is also desired and necessary. Chapter 5 describes a model for practicing this very difficult balancing act and bringing the very best of the two structures to life.

.... Chapter Five ....
Directing an Empowered, Self-Disciplined Workgroup

Introduction

Chapter 4 described the utilization of an operational structure outlined in a circular model. As discussed, it is not intended to replace the traditional organizational model but, rather, to complement it in a way that describes how we would expect the organization to function on a day-to-day basis. It moves the focus of management from one of control to one of influence and creating desired outcomes.

Some would say that the operational model would result in a lack of organizational focus and perhaps a workforce that appeared out of control. Even in this enlightened model, it is management's responsibility to provide focus and direction to the organization, instill an atmosphere of self-discipline, and at the same time, encourage empowerment within the workforce. The question isn't whether these critical considerations have importance but, rather, how they are provided within a progressively led workplace. This chapter will provide an explanation of the critical elements that make up this progressive work environment and some guidance on getting to that point within your organization.

Empowering the Workgroup

Imagine the employees in an organization occupying the inside of a circle (see Figure 5-1). They sometimes work as individuals; in organizational groups such as Functions, Divisions, or Sections; in teams of two or more; or periodically on special project teams. Employees are configured in many different ways, and they each report to work each day with their own separate "to do" list. The reality is that employees are going many different directions, all at once, together and separately, everyday.

How do leaders provide appropriate direction to a workforce in a way that encourages ideas, innovation, empowerment and change, yet communicates to the employees what the organization expects of them and generally how the leaders expect the people in the organization to function? This is accomplished by defining the perimeter of the circle by providing "organizational anchors" that keep the workforce focused and moving forward, separate perhaps, yet tied together. As Figure 5-1 points out, there are four organizational anchors that must be in place:

- A clearly defined mission and clear customer expectations.

- Shared organizational values and an understanding of the organizational culture.

- Well-managed financial resources.

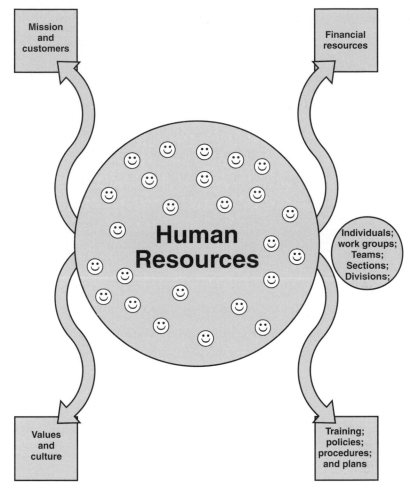

Figure 5-1. Organizational anchors are needed to keep the workforce functioning as a team.

- Appropriate levels of training; clear organizational policies; realistic standard operating procedures (SOPs); and definitive strategic and operational plans.

These anchors keep the organization from operating without focus and they provide necessary direction to all employees. Rather than controlling people by keeping them in their organizational boxes or in line, leaders have the challenge of keeping people inside the circle. There's a big difference, and it's this difference that substantially changes and enhances the leadership culture of an organization.

Within this enlightened leadership model, "bubbles" periodically form along the perimeter of the circle (see Figure 5-2). These bubbles sometimes drive managers crazy, but they shouldn't. The bubbles usually represent employees who are pushing against the perimeter of the circle. These bubbles reflect new ideas coming through the system; they can and do set the stage for change.

Much like an automobile tire with a bubble, the circle becomes somewhat unbalanced due to the "organizational bubble" that has formed. The idea, concept, or change must be addressed or processed in some way that brings closure and returns the circle to a state of balance. How is that accomplished? By assessing the anchors and determining how to proceed based on the answers to a series of questions that are asked as part of an assessment of the idea:

- Does the idea fall within the mission of the organization. or would the mission need modified?

- Is the change consistent with the organizational values? Can the current culture integrate the change internally?

- Can necessary financial resources be identified? If so, how? If not, could there be an opportunity to provide funding at a later time?

- Will employees require additional training? Do existing policies need to be modified or new policies developed

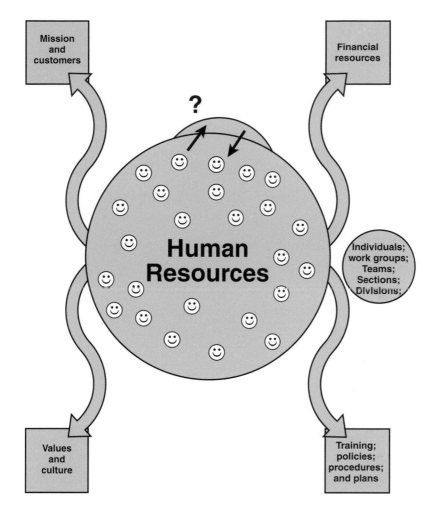

Figure 5-2. Bubbles at the perimeter or the organizational circle represent new ideas.

to accommodate the change? Do SOPs need to be developed or revised? Is the idea or change consistent with the organizations plans? Will the plans need to be modified?

Based upon this analysis, the organization can determine whether to proceed (or not proceed) with the change. Either way, the perimeter of the circle returns to round;

the bubble subsides because the idea was processed through the system and a decision was made. As one might assume, by using this assessment model, most ideas are eventually implemented in some form.

To ensure that employees stay and function inside the circle, it is important that first-level supervisors have the skills necessary to coach, counsel, and nudge as needed on a daily basis (see Figure 5-3). The term first-level supervisor, as used in this context, does not refer to a particular rank in the organizational hierarchy. It is intended to identify an individual's immediate supervisor, irrespective of rank. For instance, a nonsupervisory worker's first-level supervisor might be a foreman, while an Assistant Director's first-level supervisor would be the Director.

When second-level supervisors (or higher) must get involved in employee behavior or performance issues, the situation is usually past the stage where counseling, coaching, or nudging a person back inside the circle can be effective. In fact, when first-level supervisors fail to help their employees stay in the circle, the employees can drift so far outside acceptable norms that returning them to the organization may not be possible, and that's a shame...it really is.

First-level supervisors sometimes fail to coach, counsel, or nudge poor behavior or performance in hopes that the situation will correct itself, which seldom occurs. When employees are operating outside the circle, they are also operating without the organizational anchors that were in place to support and assist them. This is not healthy for the organization as a whole or for the worker who is in the

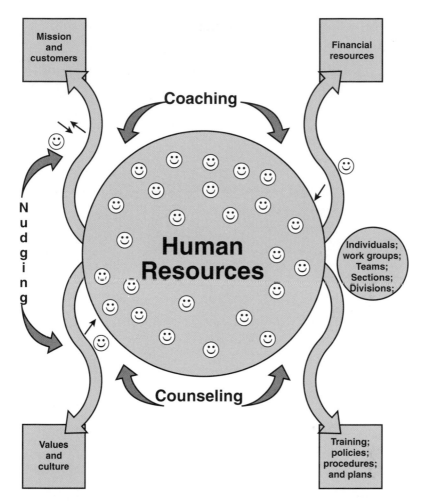

Figure 5-3. First-level supervisors must have the skills to coach, counsel, and nudge thier employees.

situation. Should the worker fail, it could have a very negative impact on the rest of the organization, including the overall organizational image.

First-level supervisors must be willing to help their employees function within the expectations established by the organizational anchors, which translates to staying inside the circle. Supervisors must be willing to coach, counsel, and nudge on a regular basis to accomplish this. The organization as a whole depends on leaders who provide focus and direction so that empowerment and self-discipline can thrive and this operational structure will serve the internal and external customers' needs.

.... Some Final Thoughts ....

This book describes organizational and individual leadership in a unique context. The two are not separate from each other and are keys to long-term success. Some specific requirements for success include:

- Clearly describing, managing, and leading all the components of the system helps members of an organization see the bigger picture and find themselves within that picture. It is important to describe the interdependency and importance of every member to the overall success of the organization in delivering the full mission.

- All supervisors and officers are responsible for functioning as positive leaders in the organization. The quality of leadership at every level affects the quality of service internally and externally. Within an environment that stresses an expectation of self-discipline, quality leadership (more than any other factor) defines the extent to which people can simultaneously develop, grow, and serve the organization.

- Organizational and operational structures do two separate (yet related) things for the system. Unless both are present, neither is fully effective. Teaching all members behavioral and performance expectations, reinforcing self-discipline, clearly documenting, and managing the organizational anchors, processing ideas and change, and providing supervision geared to coach, counsel, and nudge on a daily basis are keys to success in a progressive organization. People want direction, need focus, desire empowerment, and must be willing to exercise self-discipline to cause the organization to function most effectively.

There is really no secret to organizational development and excellence. Achieving success requires leadership, hard work, competence, open minds, mutual trust, and mutual respect among the participants. If we get up each day trying to move our systems and ourselves another step forward, we'll do better than we did the day before. Thanks for exploring this book...I hope you find the entire series helpful.

. . . . About the Author . . . .

Dennis Compton is a well-known speaker and the author of the When In Doubt, Lead! series, as well as many other articles and publications. His background includes a significant management, consulting, and teaching history covering a wide variety of disciplines and subjects in the public and private sectors.

Dennis is currently the Fire Chief in Mesa, Arizona. He previously served as Assistant Fire Chief in the Phoenix, Arizona, Fire Department. During a career that spans over thirty-one years, Chief Compton has been an active participant in the international fire service. As a result, many fire departments and other organizations have recognized his accomplishments. Among other things, he is the immediate past-chair of the Executive Board of the International Fire Service Training Association (IFSTA), chair of the Congressional Fire Services Institute's National Advisory Committee, and serves on the board of the National Fire Protection Association (NFPA). Dennis was selected as the American Fire Sprinkler Association's Fire Service Person of the Year 2000 and is a charter member of the Arizona Fire Service Hall of Fame. He was also selected as the Year 2001 Distinguished Alumnus of the Year by the University of Phoenix.

One colleague has said, "Dennis Compton has the unique ability to simplify typically complex organizational issues. He has displayed this as a visionary, educator, consultant, planner, and leader for colleges, universities, non-profit organizations, private corporations, conferences, and other organizations." His straightforward way of communicating frames a perspective that readers find simple and refreshing, yet thought provoking. We know you will enjoy this latest effort in the When in Doubt, Lead! series.

. . . . Notes . . . .

. . . . Notes . . . .

. . . . Notes . . . .